DP DESIGN

DESIGNING CHANGE

ORO EDITIONS

Publishers of Architecture, Art, and Design
Gordon Goff: Publisher

www.oroeditions.com
info@oroeditions.com

Published by ORO Editions

Graphic Design: Rebecca Jin
Text: Mike Lim, Belle Chung & Win Le Htun
ORO Project Coordinator: Kirby Anderson

10 9 8 7 6 5 4 3 2 1 First Edition

Library of Congress data available upon request. World Rights: Available

ISBN: 978-1-943532-34-6

Color Separations and Printing: ORO Group Ltd.
Printed in China.

International Distribution: www.oroeditions.com/distribution

ORO Editions makes a continuous effort to minimize the overall carbon footprint of its publications. As part of this goal, ORO Editions, in association with Global ReLeaf, arranges to plant trees to replace those used in the manufacturing of the paper produced for its books. Global ReLeaf is an international campaign run by American Forests, one of the world's oldest nonprofit conservation organizations. Global ReLeaf is American Forests' education and action program that helps individuals, organizations, agencies, and corporations improve the local and global environment by planting and caring for trees.

PROJECTS

DEFINING SPACES

A HOLISTIC APPROACH TO INTERIOR DESIGN

With a deep concern for the built environment, DP Design offers interior design, space planning and branding strategy services. Headquartered in Singapore and conceived in 1982 by Gan Eng Oon, Lydia Fong, Victor Loh and Kwan Mohyin, DP Design has in recent years delivered and presented an international body of sterling works such as Singapore's Esplanade – Theatres on the Bay; Paragon Shopping Centre; HDB Hub; Singapore Stock Exchange; Orchard Central and Resorts World Sentosa; The Dubai Mall, the world's largest shopping destination; Cinemaxx Palembang Icon, the flagship of a newly launched cinema chain in Indonesia and its associated café chain, Maxx Coffee; as well as the well-established investment bank UOB Kay Hian in Malaysia. The firm also has a hand in the interior design of Respublika Plaza Astana in Kazakhstan, a mixed development comprising retail, office and SOHO units.

The design firm takes a holistic approach to interior spaces, a direct response to a building's intrinsic architectural and formal relationships. At DP Design, interior-architects create environments that seamlessly integrate people, architecture, technology and the ultimate purpose of the space. The practice at DP Design, therefore, transcends superficial interior decoration. Its designs endeavour to preserve and enhance the natural behaviour of a building, working with project-specific materials, lighting conditions and planning techniques. In doing so, DP Design works closely with the architects during building conception, playing a critical role in helping to layout and plan the overall building so as to express and achieve specific internal conditions. Internal spaces of completed buildings, on the other hand, are re-examined and re-worked by DP Design to achieve a functionality and personality that correspond with the existing architecture.

Moreover, it is the intimate participation and exchange between DP Design's designers and architects during the formation of a building's interior design that allow a building's character and functionality to be realised to its fullest potential. Indeed, the result achieved strengthens a visitor's likelihood of identifying with it. Not only does DP Design support DP Architects in achieving a holistic design pratice, it also collaborates with other reputable architects in a highly selective pool of projects. At DP Design, every line and corner is thoroughly considered as the design teams take pride in the results of this diligence, conducting ourselves as designers.

DP Design seeks to create spaces – spaces that are memorable, relevant and sustainable with a highly dedicated team of designers, the firm seeks opportunities that display its expertise and experiences, while challenging and inspiring creative passions.

DESIGN REIMAGINED

THE SEMINAL EXHIBITION

Delving deeper into the design thought underpinning the excellence of its projects, *Designing Change* is the second title in the photographic celebration of DP Design's ever-growing portfolio. In this curation of our latest works, we highlight our engagement with the social forces of time through an examination of the relationship between spaces and the communities that they are designed for.

Space has always been important to us as an architecture-based design firm working in intimate participation and exchange with architects. The first title, *Designing Spaces*, is a curtain-raiser for our design opus, focusing on the spaces we shape and its intrinsic relation to the architectural form; the experience of this space drives the holistic design practice which is a hallmark of DP Design. Our designers are driven to look at circulation, functionality and the volumetric experience, transcending superficial interior decoration to seamlessly integrate people, architecture, technology and ultimately, purpose of the space.

The design process for every project is instilled with a form of rigour, ensuring a quality baseline from which to propel the design forward into excellence. From Esplanade – Theatres on the Bay and Singapore Dance Theatre to Resorts World Sentosa and The Dubai Mall, we believe that for any project in any typology, the difference is in the details. Committing to this mission, our team of interior-architects and designers have worked to develop and uphold the same rigour in each design progression, ensuring certain consistencies in the way every project is delivered: the refined articulation of junctions, joinery, details.

Steadfastly committed to design excellence, DP Design sails onward to meet new design challenges and milestones. Spaces, designed for people, are intrinsically variable in nature. Like its end-users, change is its constant; especially so with the onset of the fourth Industrial Revolution – Digital Disruption. Recognising this, we have raised the question: what lies beyond the designing of spaces? As an extension of the Digital Revolution (also known as the Third Industrial Revolution) which is marked by mass computerisation, the speed, scope and scale of change will be unprecedented, non-linear and massive.

We must therefore, re-question perceived boundaries, re-examine the people-space relationship and re-consider the way in which space impacts and shapes social behaviour. In doing so, our design lenses will and must shift; our strategies necessitate design for change, which moves with time. Beyond the unadulterated refinement of space – bearing in mind that there is a permanent capacity for flux in interior design – we look beyond the singular objective of spatial quality: how to use space to influence the user, and in turn how the user influences the space.

Designing Change is an introductory narrative of how design has altered social perceptions of specific spaces and therefore, social interactions within these spaces. Furthermore, changes in social behaviours and interaction has in turn affected our design of these spaces; the projects presented in this book are shaped by a variety of influences, from the social media saturating our cultural environment to the evolving definition of wellness by the tech-savvy modern traveller. We recognise in the engagement with social forces of time, the potential reformulation of design approaches for the positive transformation of a community and its social behaviour.

RETAIL

DOHA FESTIVAL CITY MALL

DOHA, QATAR

Doha Festival City Mall embodies the mix of traditional Arab customs with modern lifestyle, reflective of the measured evolution of its city into a metropolis of the Arabian Gulf region. With more than 400 international and local retail stores, it is a prime component of the largest retail and entertainment hub in Qatar. Sensitive design innovations were presented in novel forms while remaining deeply rooted in the strong history and cultural identity of the country.

Grounded in way-finding and place-making, the interior design strategised the easy identification of the various zones to break down the massive scale of the building. This is opulently encapsulated in the massive custom-made chandeliers featured in the main atriums. Each is inspired by different beautiful geometric patterns in Arabic cultures and serve not only as bespoke centrepieces, but also as distinguishing elements of the four respective retail zones.

The four zones are created with the intention of characterising specific retail segments of the mall, all made uniquely identifiable with a different theme. A star-shaped chandelier, a modern interpretation of an Islamic pattern through glass and crystal, marks the 'Luxury District' where a clean monochromatic colour palette highlights the shop fronts of high-end brands. Food and hospitality offerings in the 'Market Place' are complemented with a warm and woody material palette, conveying the sense of welcoming nature – an essence of Middle Eastern hospitality. Similarly, a different spatial tone is set at the events plaza connected to fast fashion and full-line stores, where a flexible and programmable layout takes precedence.

The intricately designed interior complements the simpler but provocative exterior that pays homage to the desert. Reimagining each retail zone as the heart of public spaces, local character is infused with contemporary way-finding design elements that lay the groundwork for self-identification and place-making. Connecting people with place, the interior design capitalises on the assets and aspirations of Doha.

women'secret
انديز
undiz
damas
COLLECTIONS

icing
SALE

The play with linearity within the expansive circular form of the skylight effectively creates visual interest as well as a notable landmark.

gamers
جيمرس

maje

EMAAR SQUARE MALL

ISTANBUL, TURKEY

A subterranean lifestyle destination, Emaar Square Mall forms the retail component of the larger Emaar Square development in Istanbul, Turkey. It comprises over 400 retail, food and beverage, and entertainment outlets. Conceptualising the mall, DP Design took an unconventional approach; designing the interior of the mall from bottom-up where three-quarters of its 150,000 square metres (four out of six levels) were built underground. The challenge then was to ensure that the mall remained attractive to tourists and locals alike, despite its unconventional setting.

The design took cues from vibrant Turkish street life to propose a system of paths as 'streets' to connect its 'plazas' and 'public squares', forming an underground retail empire resplendent with movement and activity. Navigation through the retail corridors is made easier via clear way-finding strategy and concept, inspired by the four seasons of Istanbul. It not only visually established four individualised zones, but also creates a unique retail experience. Copper hues and crystalline silvers in the material palette represent autumn and winter respectively, while the summer theme is portrayed by water imageries and blues in tandem with the aquarium housed in the zone. Similarly, the central sunken courtyard, located in the spring zone, presents an enticing view to the visitors above with its bright ambiance and delightful use of greenery. This is a peek into the retail splendour below and also a culmination of the strategies to blur the boundaries between external and internal.

By respecting the everyday environment in Istanbul through the interpretation of local identity in the spatial sequences with distinct nodes and views, the mall becomes a meaningful and delightful environment. Inviting and intriguing – Emaar Square Mall encourages visitors to rediscover the spirit of exploration in vibrant bazaar activities and shopping.

GALERIES LAFAYETTE

OME
BIR KEREDE
BIR KAREDE
EMAAR
SQUARE
MALL

The mall's central sunken plaza operates as a constantly active theatre for people-watching and a multipurpose space with outdoor dining around an interactive water feature, which can be transformed into an ice-skating rink in the winter.

PIDEM

TURKISH VILLAGE

KASAP DÖNER

LOVE

ion SKY
Welcome!
Singapore's unique cityscape surrounds us, the sky is constantly changing, and spectacular clouds float past the windows everyday.
Enjoy the view!

ION SKY

SINGAPORE

A multidimensional observation deck, Ion Sky presents an experiential journey with its panoramic views of the unique cityscape of Singapore. Set on the 55th floor of the Ion Orchard shopping centre in the heart of Orchard Road, the observation gallery was redesigned to achieve experiential aspirations. It is divided into three phases – Holding Area, Transitional Space and The Canopy, in which the journey unfolds through immersive storytelling via multi-media LED screens and projection imagery.

The Holding Area appeals to modern day social media culture by offering an 'Instagrammable' space. Here, visitors can begin to document their visual expedition. A large LED media wall acts as the filmic primer. It is accompanied by cloud projections on the ceiling from which a bespoke centre-piece mimicking foliage is suspended – alluding to the name of the observation gallery. As the background canvas, the interior material palette is elegant and light, accented with polished-metal finishes. Transitioning to the final destination above, the mirrored lift cars are fitted with OLED displays. These create a cinematic dimension, enhancing the ascent to The Canopy via various videography exhibits. The Canopy space is equipped with over 13 metres of full-height walls, panoramic projections and blackout blinds along the perimeter of the deck; serving as a canvas for a 360-degree media show. At the end of this visual journey, the blackout blinds roll up simultaneously to reveal the shimmering Singapore and Orchard skyline.

Ion Sky may not be the highest observation point in Singapore; but DP Design has engaged visitors by creating in novel spatial environment, transforming the simple pleasure of seeing the city into a captivating experience.

ion SKY

UNI QLO
THE COFFEE BEAN & TEA LEAF
からだ想いごはん
大戸屋
OOTOYA
Japanese Restaurant
We are located at Orchard Central #08-012

ORCHARD CENTRAL A&A

SINGAPORE

Espousing the architectural focus of linking private commercial space with its public environs, the internal programming of Orchard Central emphasises connectivity within its multilevel retail. Sited at the corner of the Orchard Road shopping district, the exploratory circulation of the first vertical shopping centre in Singapore shifts the urban walkway indoors, enticing movement through the stretched vertical dimension.

The central atrium splices the elongated footprint of the building, maximising essential sight lines to the upper floors. It comprises a five-storey rock-climbing wall, lighting features and graphics encompassing multiple floors, as well as a myriad of suspended artworks that draw the eye up the activated core. Far from a typical internal mall atrium, it emulates an external plaza and acts as an urban thoroughfare. To further establish the visual link, the upper floors protrude into the atrium in staggered sculptural forms, creating interest and ensuring additional displays of shop-fronts. Inversely, shoppers on upper levels can overlook different activity hubs at the plaza below as a natural ground reference. Lighting systems and linear ceiling patterns put further emphasis on the spatial element of verticality and reduce the monotony of extensive overhead floor-plates.

With accessibility as crucial a task as visibility, all 52 escalators and 12 glass elevators follow the simple criterion of being highly visible and simple to access. This allows shoppers to weave through efficient paths between floors, manipulating the natural tendency to move horizontally. One of six super escalators direct external pedestrian traffic from the corner of Orchard Road straight to the fourth floor. The various atriums created by the escalators overlook cafes, lounge seating and dining areas, presenting vantage points to social interactions.

Communicating a new type of shared space through its visual and physical interchanges, Orchard Central is fuelled with life and activity, vitalising the streetscape.

AWARDS

2015 Singapore Good Design Mark Awards

MINION CAKES
AVAILABLE HERE
COLD STONE

HAPPY
HOUR
ASAHI
DRAFT
BEER
$9.00
BUY 2 GET 1 FREE
HOUSE SAKE
WINE

SANDBOX
POKÉ LULU

Doing away with the conventional central atrium, the 'Discovery Walk' zone effectively becomes an extended living room where consumers stroll, shop, rest, watch, wait and read.

Here, the delightful marriage of form and function is evident as clusters of different retail themes are designed with varied overlapping volumes and distinctive interior architecture that adopts a series of rectilinear elements.

LifeWear.
Simple made better.
からだ想いごはん
大戸屋
OOTOYA
Japanese Restaurant
We are located at
Orchard Central
#08-012

UNIQLO
THE SOCIAL FOOT
HENRI CHARPENT

PROJECT KEIKO

KOBE, JAPAN

Project Keiko sits in an in-between zone beneath a hotel and adjacent to two train stations. Utilised by transient commuters and pedestrians, it formerly offered simple retail options such as a supermarket, tailor shops and sundries. In an effort to reinvest in this transition space, DP Design was engaged to purposefully redesign for a retail mall that capitalises on its location and connectivity.

The design strategy was grounded in maximising the usage of public spaces and focused on rerouting the circulation to best enhance visibility and access to the retail selections. The mall was given a proper central atrium by repositioning the central escalator, which not only generates a sense of place among end-users, but also improves sightlines; thus enhancing the focal point and visual accessibility of where social activies take place. Simultaneously, the urban thoroughfare running through the mall, which links the nearby Shinkansen station with the surrounding neighbourhood, was recognised as a corridor of opportunity to fashion a valued public space that encourages social interaction and movement. Acknowledging the budget constraints, existing elements such as railings and floorings were retained; while colours and greenery were introduced. Additionally, public amenities were upgraded as part of the goal of creating a more 'dwellable' urban corridor where people can easily enter, enjoy and leave.

By creating well-defined routes, movement and sightlines, the design aims to encourage social, economic and environmental benefits. Social activity is promoted by an increased sense of ownership through a well-designed public space. This draws patrons to the mall and ultimately achieves the goal of rejuvenating commercial activity in a unique space.

Avenue

RESTAURANTS

TOFU KITCHEN MAME no HATAKE

PLQ
MALL

PLQ MALL

SINGAPORE

The PLQ Mall is the retail supplement of the larger people-centric mixed-development, Paya Lebar Quarter. Sited adjacent to Paya Lebar MRT station and the long-standing Malay settlement of Geylang Serai, its design serves to form a contextual relationship with the socio-economic fabric of its environs. This is clearly and concisely articulated in the songket-inspired (a traditional malay brocade) weave pattern on its façade.

The aesthetic language is then carried into the interiors where it is expressed in various permutations for a consistent and coherent design. The basement and upper storeys of the mall feature a similar but unique expression of the motif as a ceiling feature or floor pattern, making them easily identifiable. The lattice motif also serves a functional purpose, enabling a cost-effective solution for fire safety regulations and M&E requirements.

Strategising clear definition of space, the design of this suburban mall emphasised space planning, functionality and simple navigation as a complement to the pedestrian-oriented nature of the commercial hub. Its public plaza, which doubles as an events space for the community, allows seamless access at ground level and draws pedestrians through the development.

PLQ Mall is an urban marker – a focal point integrating various users from the adjacent office, residential and transit developments – thereby encouraging serendipitous interactions and relationships. Ultimately, it aims to forge a sense of community and identity.

NOW OPEN
#03-08
NOW OPEN
#03-08

樂天皇朝
PARADISE DYNASTY
#03-08

SHAW CENTR
LIFT LOBBY

SHAW CENTRE

SINGAPORE

Located along Orchard Road, Singapore's most famous shopping precinct, Shaw House and Shaw Centre are adjacent, interconnected developments by the same developer, consisting of a shopping mall and two office buildings. Undertaking the A&A works to the public areas and lobbies of the mall and offices, DP Design recognised the overarching identity of the complex as the home of a major cinema and a departmental anchor store, where its other spaces have become supplementary elements often overlooked. Centering the design strategy on the potential of the undermined spaces, this A&A project was an exercise in the subtle shaping of user perspective through the refinement of their spatial environment.

An intimate shopping experience was first recreated by cultivating a warm hospitality ambiance, with a strong visual character of structured linear elements juxtaposed against organic curves and wood-grained textures. Despite the constraints of an existing circulation and layout, interior elements were purposefully pieced together to achieve a consistent design language permeating the refurbished areas. Through the establishment of a clear visual identity for the circulatory arteries of the complex, patrons are influenced to perceive the entirety of the development as a whole. Intricacies of lighting, scale, materiality and colour were played on to differentiate functional and spatial variations, all the while maintaining a singular identity in the progression through the different public zones of the development, from retail areas to office lobbies.

Undertaking the challenge of using space to influence user patterns, DP Design positively transforms the volumetric experience of the interiors in a cohesive design concept, ultimately rejuvenating commercial activities.

EXIT

L2
POLO
RALPH LAUREN

LAW CENTRE
LIFT LOBBY
LIFT
LOBBY A

SHAW CEN
Shaw House
EXIT
IMAX

SINGPOST CENTRE

SINGAPORE

In this extension to the existing Singapore General Post Office, an increased retail component measuring a gross floor area of 25,000sqm explores the new platform of Online and Offline Retail. This includes a supermarket in the basement, eight cinema halls, a food court and a playground on the roof garden. Taking direction from digital connectivity which gave rise to the innovative amalgamation of online retail services in the General Post Office, the design focuses on the nuances of connection: the aesthetic cohesiveness between the new and the old design elements, as well as the social connectivity experienced.

Espousing the fundamentals of the Modernist architectural language of the existing building, the retail extension is harmonised with the existing through the disciplined articulation of uncluttered silhouettes and strong contrasts. Machine-milled profiles and contemporary raw materials are detailed to express a clean industrial chic canvas. The disciplined, minimal aesthetics are a nod to the current digital age, providing new branding for some of the retail tenants including the General Post Office.

The existing open plaza melds into the retail extension at various points via interconnected public spaces and multi-level visual linkages. This effectively transforms the existing singular platform plaza into an integrated, purposeful one. For instance, skylights opening up to the roof garden allow retail tenants centred along the indoor atrium to enjoy natural sunlight and a visual relation to the outdoor community plaza above. This multi-level hub of social activity becomes the focal point of the circulatory channels, revelling in its spatial relationships.

Today, the SingPost Centre is a noteworthy commercial hub and a vibrant social space, with the contemporary image of its General Post Office spearheading the digital retail and customer service experiences.

ARAB

01

BEVERAGE
100% Chargrilled
PREMIUM ANGUS BEEF
SALE

MARUGAME
UDON
UDON & TEMPURA

TRANS STUDIO MALL

JAKARTA, INDONESIA

Located south of Jakarta in Cibubur, Trans Studio Mall introduces the concept of an integrated lifestyle entertainment hub. Not only offering an unparalleled dining and shopping experience, the mall also has an integrated theme park along with an adjoining hotel tower, Hotel Mercure.

Inspired by the traditional Indonesian Cendrawasih dance that was originally derived from the Bird of Paradise known as *burung cendrawasih*, strong yet soft curvatures are placed throughout the mall. The interior mimics the male and female dancers' identities, dividing plots into their unique spaces while still complementing each other through details for a cohesive whole. Unlike the usual shopping mall, a glass dome which acts as an observatory deck is placed in the middle of the atrium. A playscape-netting feature surrounds the dome, allowing shoppers to interact with the space.

TORICO

andrew

HOSPITALITY

NOVOTEL SINGAPORE ON STEVENS

SINGAPORE

AWARDS

2019 IDCS Interior Design Excellence Awards
Best Hospitality Design ≥ 201 Rooms
(Gold)

2018 BCI Asia Interior Design Award
Hospitality – Singapore
(Winner)

DRIVEN x DESIGN Melbourne Design Awards
(Gold)

DRIVEN x DESIGN London Design Awards
Interior Design – International Hospitality
(Silver)

Despite the built landscape of the present day, associating with natural elements and green spaces are instrumental to a person's physical and mental well-being. Inherently attuned to nature, humans as highly social creatures and they thrive on positive interactions in such spatial environments. The design approach the hospitality project embraces this holistic view of wellness by shaping spaces which best inspire interaction, all the while immersing guests in an oasis of calm. In the same spirit as its architecture – conceptualised in and characterised by the Chinese character *ren* meaning 'people' – the interior was designed with the well-being of people in mind.

Aesthetic nuances form a storytelling thread throughout the hotel. Stepping stone ornaments lead into the entrance lobby, which was conceptualised as a dynamic communal space. Rather than serving only passive check-in and waiting functions, the lobby also showcases the drinks and noodle bars which double up as co-working meeting facilities. With the creative thought firmly centred on people, the all-day dining opens up to the pool deck during fine weather, encouraging social activities and the concept of natural living. All other main function areas, such as lobbies and meeting facilities, capitalise on the lush landscaping by extending to the outside, forming relationships between different spaces and presenting the notion of seamlessness between the internal and external.

The interconnected and complementary architectural, interior and landscape concept behind the larger Novotel & Mercure Singapore development produces a cohesive experience of rest and green respite. A sense of community is fostered in the delightful and memorable co-living spaces, achieving the social goal of the design and inventively articulating the ethos of the hospitality brand.

The breakout space is a highly active social space featuring a ceiling mimicking a tree canopy, while another ceiling design is reminiscent of the starlight of a pine forest, acting as the highlight along the corridor into the ballroom and meeting rooms.

redpan

REDPAN

SINGAPORE

Food is sustenance. It is also a powerful connector. Bonds, built through commensality, were observed in the informal discussions held by DP staff at nearby cafes, where the intimacy and chemistry fostered between staff spills over into the workplace. re**dp**an was thus conceived as an exercise in building camaraderie through a fun local dining experience, in an urbane environment where the distinctions between work, rest and play are blurred.

The 'red' in the restaurant's name represents the fully Singaporean labour of love, while 'pan' refers to the culinary essential where two very different industries – design and food – can cook up a creative storm together. re**dp**an deliberates on the place-making ingredients which bring together people, drawing on the elements of food, play and nature.

The interior concept was refined to one core design element of generous curves, purposefully contoured to create a playful atmosphere that establishes conviviality and a sense of relaxation on an intuitive level. This understated spatial language highlights the depth of design thought undertaken in the exploration of materials and craftsmanship – from the stacked unfinished plywood which revels in the authenticity of the material, to the hanging glass feature comprising 2,000 manually adjusted pieces, as well as the showcase of the versatility of glass in a custom-designed meeting table. The fluidity of the curves is key to the openness of the space; despite its location in a shopping mall, there is an ever-present visual connection to nature. The open layout ensures unblocked window views to greenery, while a free-standing dining area is strategically planned under a skylight to evoke the feel of an alfresco terrace. The result is a chic and vibrant communal space that appeals without extravagance.

re**dp**an began as a simple wish to share good food in a good setting. It is a 'living room' where ideas are exchanged over a cosy meal. Beyond offering inventive Singaporean cuisine to working professionals, it is a memorable gathering ground that anchors relationships and nurtures creativity, enriching the human experience.

AWARDS

2017 Prix Versailles
Asie du Sud et Pacifique Restaurants

2016 IDCS Interior Design Excellence Awards
– F&B Design
(Bronze)

EXIT
REDPAN

REDPAN
ELEKTRA

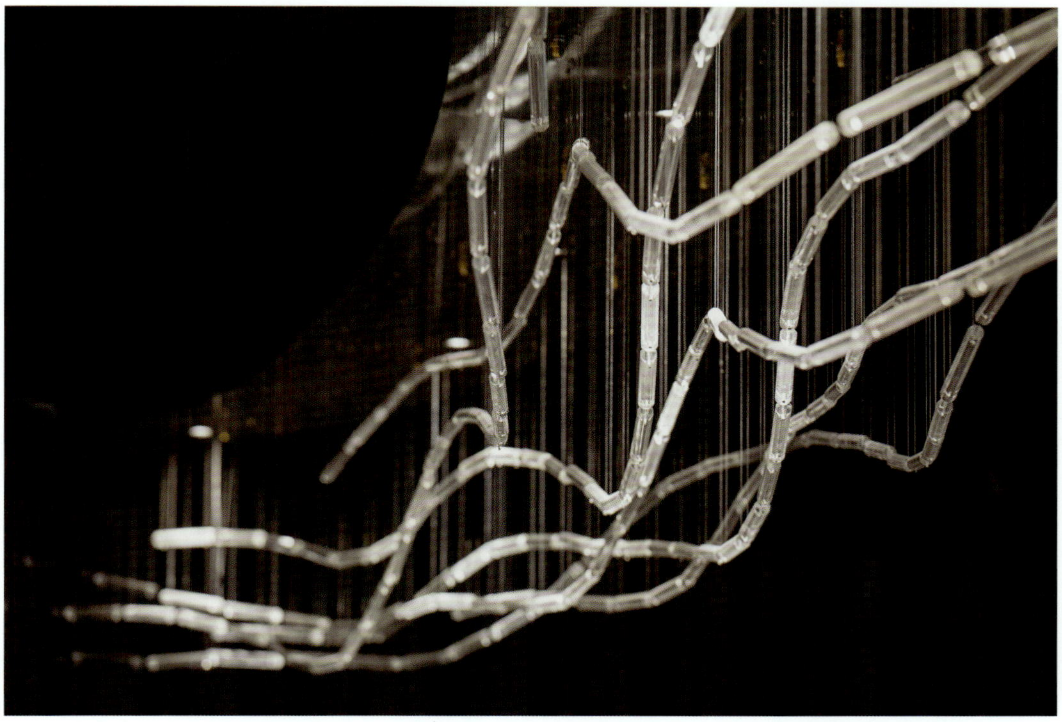

To create a multi-functional space that is warm and vibrant while conveying a sense of chic without relying on extravagant decoration and furnishing, the concept was distilled down to one core design element – generous curves and rounded corners that add sophistication, dynamism and softness to a functional design.

redpan

SINGAPORE AIRLINES SILVERKRIS LOUNGE

INCHEON INTERNATIONAL AIRPORT MAIN TERMINAL

INCHEON, SOUTH KOREA

What does 'home' mean to Singaporeans and travellers?
In conceptualising the SilverKris Lounge in Incheon, the DP Design team re-examined the definition of home and presented a design scheme that elevated the 'home away from home' hospitality concept.

While maintaining the signature feel of SilverKris lounges, existing items were re-interpreted with a contemporary twist; motifs were elegantly incorporated into the lighting design and complemented by a cooler colour palette than the traditional template. The centrepiece is the heart of the social space, recognising human connection and people-watching as an integral part of the travelling experience. A feature service bar was introduced between the 'dining' and 'living' area for a stronger definition of different spaces.

Catering to travellers with shorter transit times, the design introduces a new space – a luxurious fit-out of the traditional Southeast Asia café serving coffee and local delights. The cakes in glass drawers and hand-printed tiles are immediately identifiable with Singapore, nurturing a familiar, warm ambiance of home. This Food & Beverage concept is particularly prevalent in and often associated with Singapore. By incorporating this pioneering addition to SilverKris lounges, the design anchors its international lounges with its home-grown identity while offering end-users a nostalgic imagery of home.

Accepting the challenge of not deviating from the distinctive hospitality concept of the client, the entire spatial experience was thoughtfully tailored to meet the present needs of travellers while delivering an authentic experience of Singapore.

SilverKris
Lounge

YOTEL SINGAPORE

SINGAPORE

The evolving definition of wellness is to be explored through design for the wellness-conscious traveller of today. Moving beyond the conventional expectation of luxurious amenities, the modern hotel guest – almost certain to be tech-savvy – equates efficiency and accessibility to comfort and relaxation. Key to an improved overall well-being is eco-friendliness, which is perceived as having positive effects through the reduction of negative impacts on the environment and therefore, health. To this end, Yotel Singapore delivers convenience, sustainability in design and artistic spaces by focusing on function and technology.

The tailored hospitality concept navigates spatial constraints in a confined, high-density urbanscape by manipulating visual perspective; space and depth are created through strategizing volumetric height. Site limitations are further resolved by cleverly inversing the conventional placement of the bathroom and guestroom, greeting the guest with an unexpected spatial expanse upon entry. Smart features are articulated into the design to maximise both luxury and affordability. This includes a 'Tech Wall' and an automatic adaptable bed in the hotel rooms, fully-automated self-check-ins and robot butlers. The utilisation of technology for optimal comfort encompasses the efficient building systems – detailed in informative panel displays at public areas, awareness is raised on the sustainable practices which contribute to the overall health of hotel patrons.

Aside from technological innovation and digital connectivity, the ease of offline interaction as another component of wellness is met by open co-living spaces geared towards enhancing a sense of community. All-day dining facilities blend and overlap with the pool and gym areas to create opportunities for informal work meetings and social gatherings, blurring the spatial boundaries between the elements of work and play.

The research and application of technological trends to hospitality spaces is a prime example of how DP Design strives to understand present needs and meet them. Through this astute consideration of the wellness philosophy in relation to the hotel identity and guest profile, Yotel Singapore is designed to lead the way in optimising travel experience.

AWARDS

2019 IDCS Interior Design Excellence Awards
Best Hospitality Design ≥ 201 Rooms
(Silver)

2018 BCI Asia Interior Design Awards
Hospitality
(Merit)

GET TO KNOW YOTEL
IN 5 MINUTES.

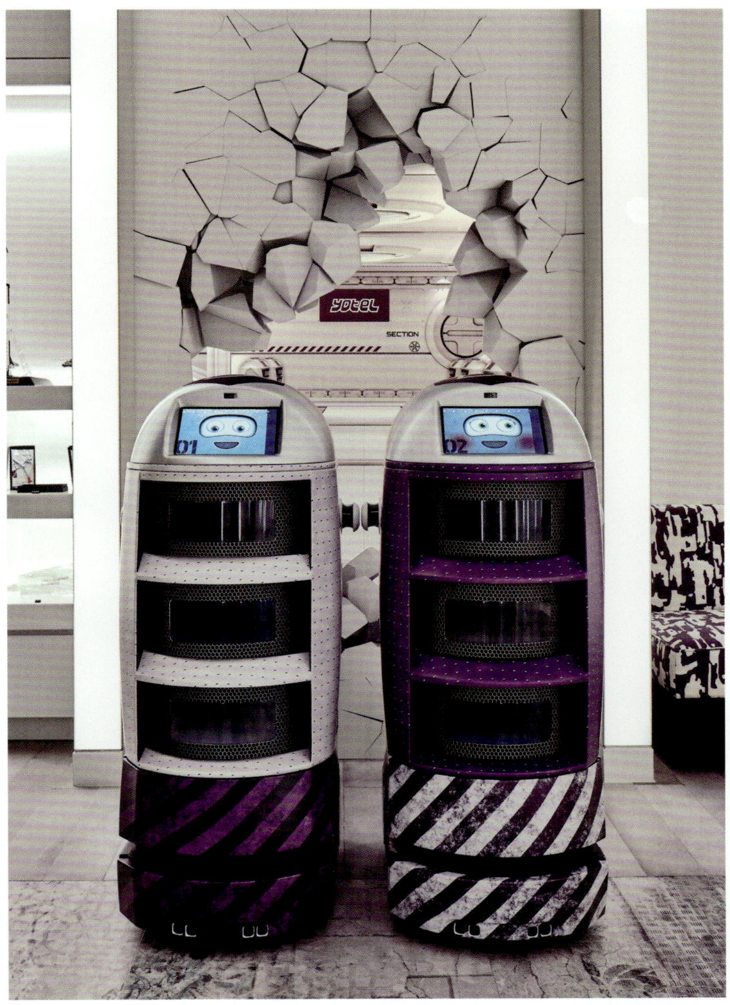

WORK, PLAY, EAT, DRINK, SLEEP, REPEAT...

INSTITUTIONAL

LEE KONG CHIAN SCHOOL OF MEDICINE

NOVENA & NTU CAMPUS, SINGAPORE

Housed in two separate campuses – the Experimental Medicine Building at Nanyang Technological University and the Clinical Sciences Building at Health City Novena – the Lee Kong Chian School of Medicine offers an ideal creative learning environment for students and researchers to engage in cross-disciplinary interaction, sharing and skills acquisition. The identity of the institution and its core pedagogy of Team-Based Learning strongly influenced its design through a blend of visual branding and functional design that conveys the institution's core purpose.

Across both campuses, social interaction and collaboration formed the key design goal and strategy. All learning spaces were designed to be flexible so as to respond to evolving and emerging user needs. In lecture situations, students are taught as an entire cohort in large-group interactive seminars or split into smaller groups. Thus the Learning Studio, Seminar Rooms and Alcove Clusters, cater to large groups with interior fit-outs that allow the space to be subdivided so as to facilitate small team-based settings. For instance, the alcoves were planned to cluster around a central space, where an instructor would address all students. Each alcove is separated from its neighbour by a counter or low cabinet; and when small group discussions ensue, blinds can be lowered at each counter to further and visually separate one alcove from another. In the case of the Research Laboratories, facilities are characterised by a triple-volume internal atrium space that serves as a break-out area, enhancing vertical mobility and provide visual linkage between multiple floors of labs. Each thoughtful, aesthetic-design accent works to create a conducive academic environment for social connectivity and knowledge exchange.

A signature uniform look for both campuses was adopted for visual consistency to foster a better sense of connection among the students and faculty. Each element – palette, lines, surfaces and materiality – comes together to present a highly sophisticated campus befitting of a leading medical school. The school's corporate colours of purple and grey in the interior colour palette accentuate the sense of identity; while recycling and preservation of boulders, tree trunks and roots removed from the construction site were incorporated in the design as sculptural displays or conversion into seating benches.

AWARDS

2018 BCI Asia Interior Design Awards
Schools – Singapore
(Winner)

LEE KONG CHIAN NTU CAMPUS

Triple-volume internal atrium spaces within the building facilitate vertical mobility and visual connection between the multiple floors of offices and laboratories. These spaces also encourage students and researchers to dwell and collaborate, spurring innovation and creative thinking.

The clean and disciplined aesthethics of the various breakout spaces is a visual iteration of the school's medical practice. Adorned with art murals and complemented by warm materials, the space is imbued with an inviting ambiance that provides psychological relief for its students.

LEE KONG CHIAN NOVENA CAMPUS

SUN MON TUE WED THU FRI SAT

TAMPINES REGIONAL LIBRARY

OUR TAMPINES HUB

SINGAPORE

People-centric and championing the ethos of integration, Our Tampines Hub (OTH) is a pioneering model of Singapore's largest integrated community, sports and lifestyle hub. It aligns the needs of 12 main stakeholders from public agencies and empowered Tampines residents to take ownership of the space through an extensive participatory design framework. The design process explored alternative spatial organisations by re-examining operation dynamics to bring diverse programmes together in a meaningful manner.

Carrying this forward into the design of the regional library, facilities and their respective stakeholders have been clustered by their programmatic relationships; the varied nature of the programmes and innovative layout required special attention in design to mitigate their intrinsically different requirements. Simultaneously, the interior design played upon thematic design elements and differentiated material to create distinct environments that maximise the sense of ownership and comfort. For example, the cooking and dining studio independently managed by the community centre is co-located with the culinary section as related spaces of learning. The studios are designed to showcase the activities within, forming an exhibit of interest not typically seen in libraries and encouraging participation across different user groups.

Embodying the synergistic design approach and strategy of the development, the design of the regional library effectively iterates the core desire of the community for a truly integrated and inclusive community destination.

AWARDS

2019 BCA Universal Design Mark Award
(Platinum)

2018 DRIVEN x DESIGN London Design Awards
Interior Design – International Public or Institutional
(Silver)

Global Architecture and Design Awards
(Honourable Mention)

FX* International Interior Design Awards
(Finalist)

2017 IDCS Interior Design Excellence Awards
Best Public Design – Asia Pacific
(Silver)

BCA Universal Design Mark Award
(GoldPLUS)

EXIT
22
24
21
31
30
EXIT

CONCEPTS
L3 16
Concepts
L3 35
L3 36

大字大图童谣
谜语300
成语故事
儿歌
成语故事
最爱天天读
智慧故事

COMICS
TERRACE ON 4

Interstitial spaces – large programmatic stairs and green niches – act as thresholds between the different age-group themes, creating shared spaces for alternative reading environments or spontaneous social interactions.

TEENS
FICTION

L2 7
Cookery

SINGAPORE
L5 39
Singapore
49

导诊台 Registration

PERENNIAL INTERNATIONAL SPECIALIST MEDICAL CENTRE

CHENGDU, CHINA

The building for the Perennial International Specialist Medical Centre in Chengdu was initially slated to be a shopping mall before developers shifted its intended purpose to healthcare, in response to market needs. Construction works for a retail outfit was well under way when DP Design rose to the challenge of redesigning an uplifting patient-centric healthcare experience within its site constraints.

Reassessing the wider design approach for healthcare, DP Design sought to achieve more than an adaptation of its existing plans to accommodate conventional healthcare strategies. Evaluating the added complexity of the project as an asset, the possible advantages for user experience that could be drawn from the original retail purpose were identified in the existing layout. The central atrium in the former shopping mall layout – purposed as a central node of activity as well as an inter-floor visual linkage – was retained with the same functional objectives in the new specialist medical centre. By programming all circulatory paths, departments and clinics around it, the atrium was proposed to be the central core of circulation, thereby allowing straightforward way-finding and easy accessibility. A café is strategically located in the atrium as a visual celebration of social connectivity, surrounded by lounge seatings for refreshments and respite. Through serving as more than an orthodox waiting area for visitors, the spatial void anchors the entire space by means of spatial programming and visual connection.

Cues from the hospitality industry were also selectively implemented to convey a warmth and sense of comfort in the medical centre. Generous usage of warm lighting, bronze colour tones and textured materiality were balanced against clean lines and elements of order, creating an oasis of relaxation that subtly expressed a quality of reassuring professionalism. Thoughtful design accents such as murals of local flowers further contribute to the atmosphere of positivity while alluding to the site context of the development.

Through the re-examination of healthcare concepts by building on frameworks from other design typologies, the Perennial International Specialist Medical Centre is a showcase of possibilities in design centred on people and their aspirations.

AWARDS

2018	IIDA Best of Asia Pacific Design Awards Healthcare (Winner)

城市候机厅
Transit Lounge
出口（往成都东站西广场）
Exit (To Chengdu East Station)
落客点
Drop-off Point

L2
妇科
肿瘤科
L2 商务中心
药房

心血管科 Cardiovascular
妇科 Gynecology
导诊台

The warm and comfortable yet professional interiors of the medical centre draws from the hospitality typologies' home-away-from-home framework.

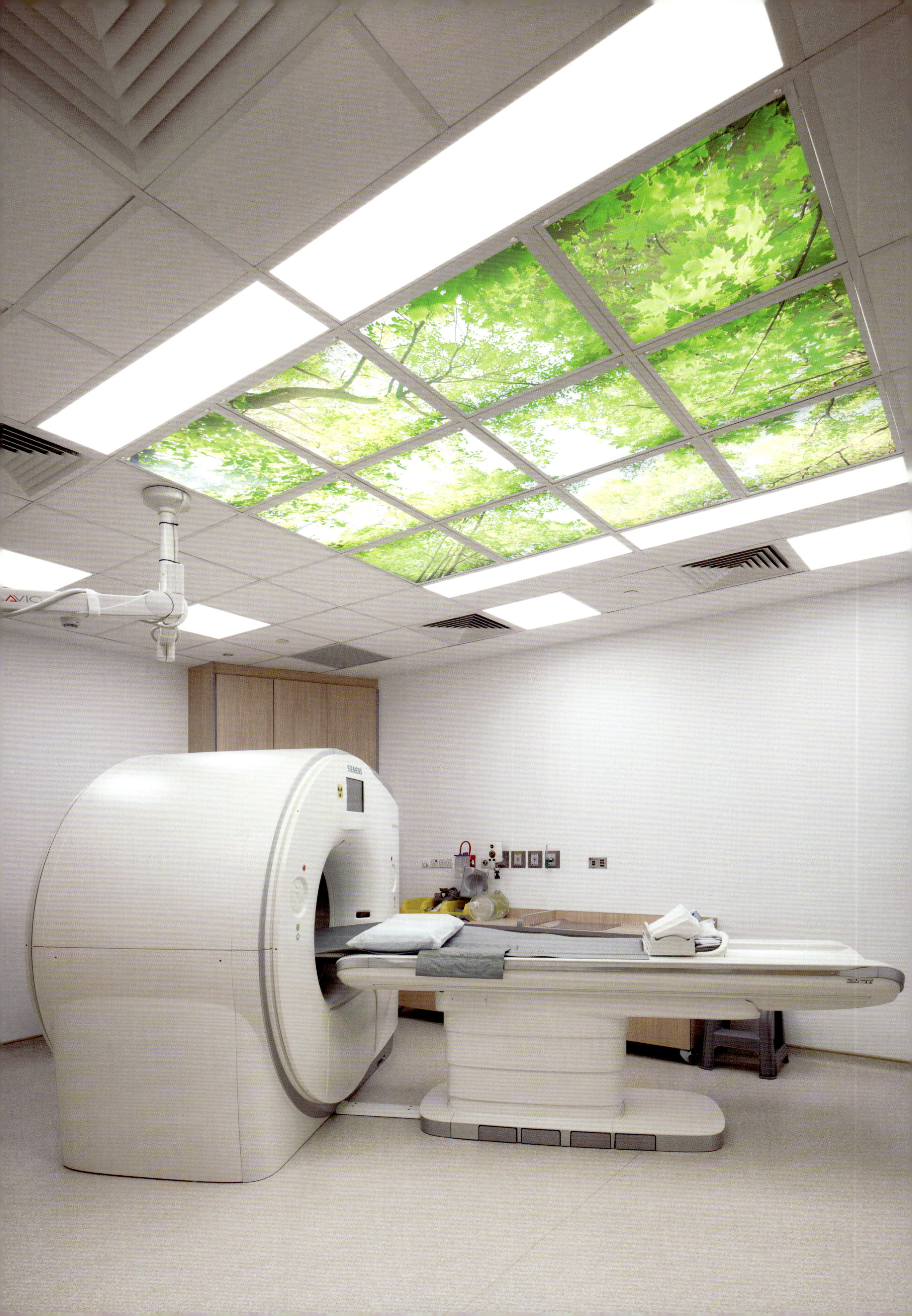
SIEMENS

SENGKANG HOSPITAL CAMPUS

SINGAPORE

An integrated regional hospital comprising a general hospital, a community hospital and specialised outpatient clinics, Sengkang Hospital Campus was designed to be a holistic and cohesive development that prioritises patients and promotes collaboration between healthcare departments, respectively. To achieve the former, the design engages in a contextual relationship with the socio-economic fabric of Sengkang, in order to build a welcoming campus enhancing the recovery process; while the latter was realised through clear but synergistic spatial programming and efficient way-finding strategies.

A monochromatic material selection – both tactile and visual, makes for a practical and timeless canvas. This careful and seamless treatment of internal and external zones effectively but gently blurs the spatial lines between private and public domains. Complementing the architectural porosity in its open spaces and public concourses, clear and efficient way-finding was key to creating connectivity between the hospital and the community it serves.

In addition to aiding in navigation, colour was skilfully employed to convey warmth and comfort. Highly social facilities such as training rooms and auditoriums celebrated the rich use of warm colours to incite a sense of community. Murals provide cheer and patterned bedheads add an element of hospitality in patient rooms. Warm lighting is generously used in public areas and implemented where appropriate in areas with technical facilities. The option of warm lighting here provides comfort to the patients before and after medical procedures.

The people-focused spatial environment of Sengkang Hospital Campus de-stigmatises the impression of a healthcare facility as a sterile, dreary place to be avoided. Its numerous plazas and concourses double as a route for residents to other places; numerous community events have been hosted within the development. In totality, the key design intent achieved a communal, inclusive environment for patients, staff and visitors alike.

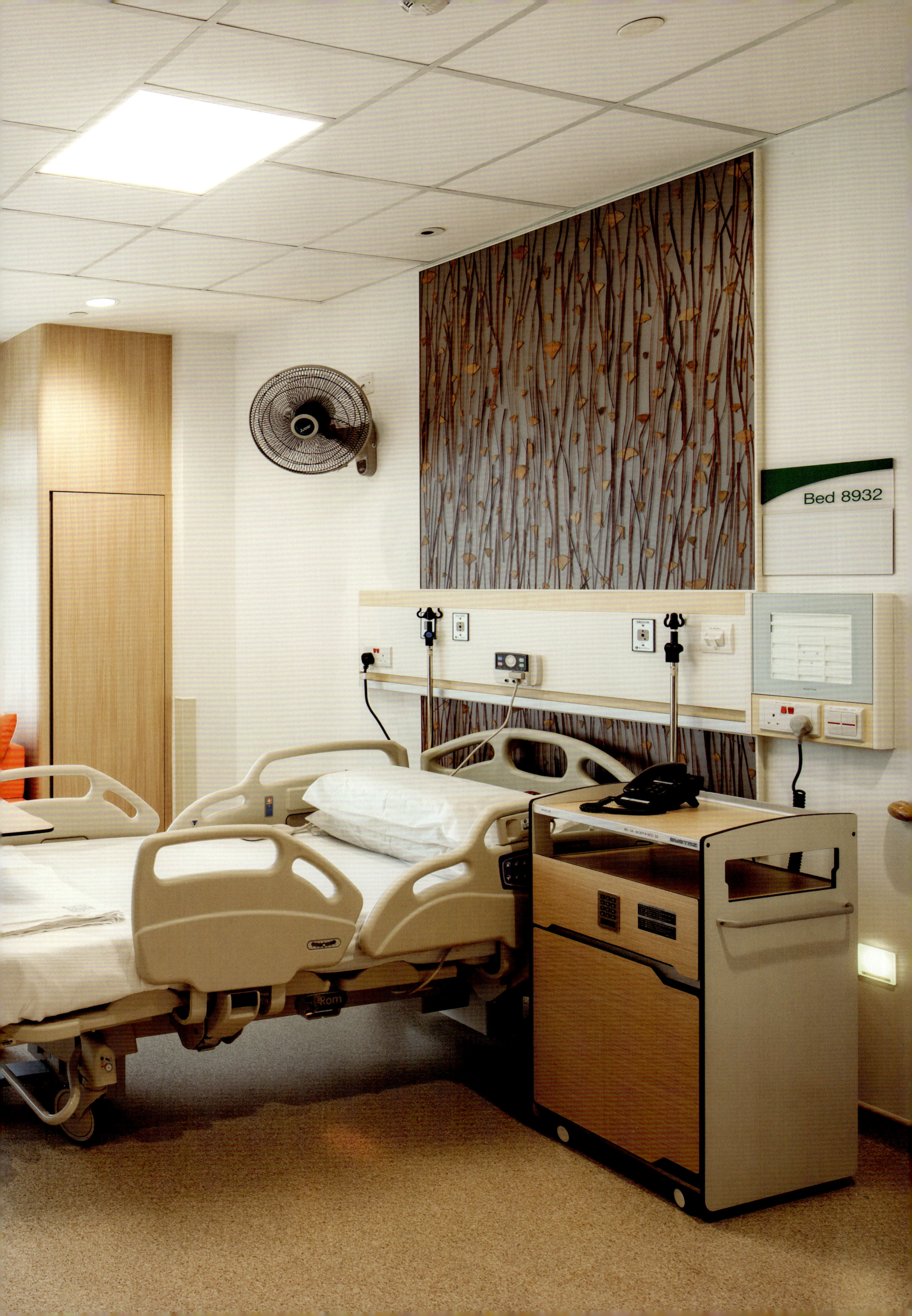
Bed 8932

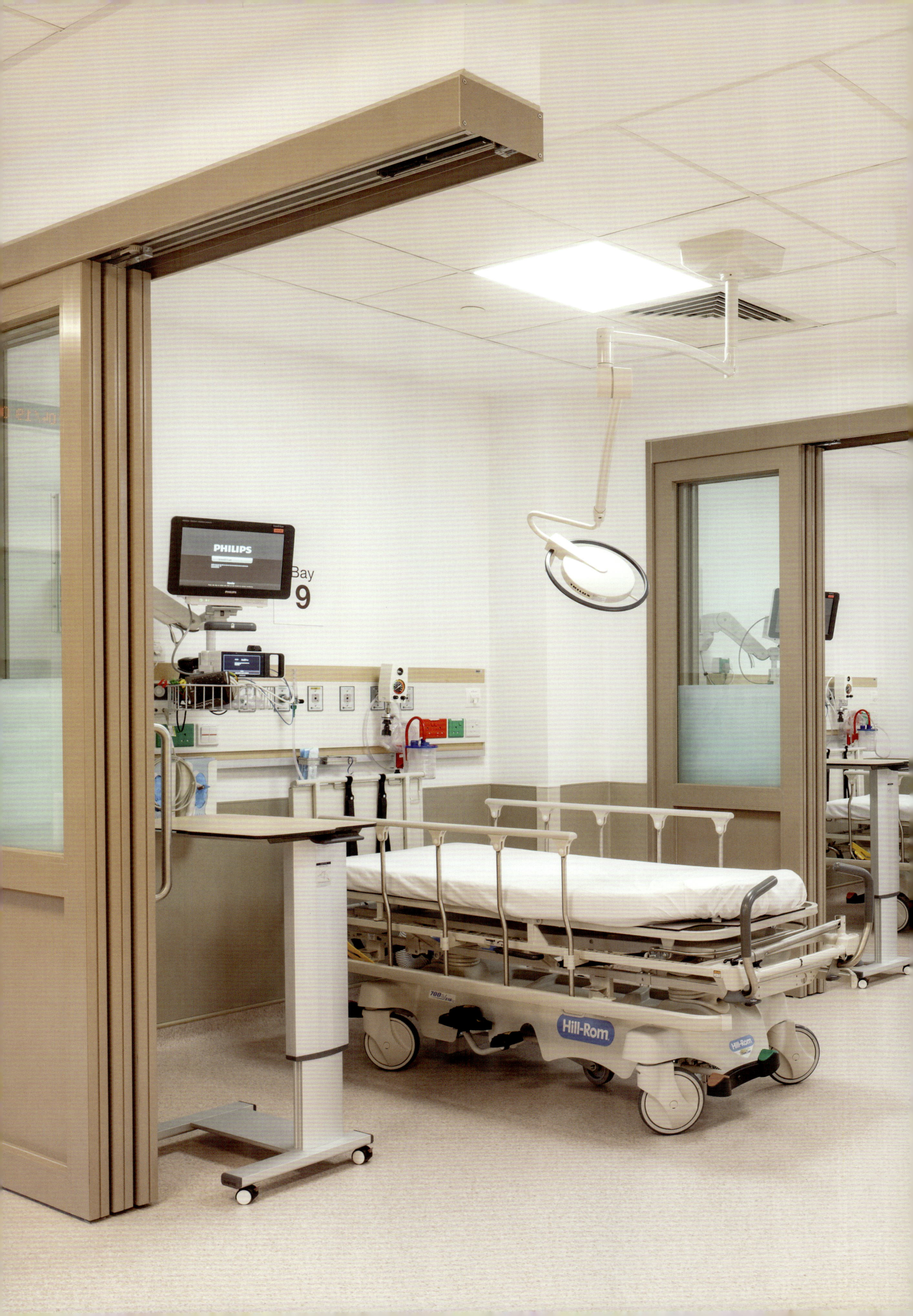

PHILIPS
Bay
9
Hill-Rom

Day Room

The complexity of systems coming together in the extensive campus required coherent signage, achieved in the simplicity of colour use. To highlight key service areas such as entrance foyers, reception desks and lobbies, bold splashes of colour draw attention to social spaces such as lounge areas and rest seating.

EXIT

EXIT

RESIDENTIAL

FENDI

ALPHA HILL

HO CHI MINH CITY, VIETNAM

Compact but luxurious, functional yet delightful – Alpha Hill was designed to be the epitome of high-end residential living in the high-density metropolis of Ho Chi Minh City. Comprising two- and three-bedroom micro units, its spatial constraint was a challenge that provided DP Design with the opportunity to explore new design possibilities.

The vibrant and successful living spaces of the residences in Alpha Hill began with the vision for community, and a deep understanding of cultural and environment needs of the locals. In doing so, the design exploration sought to define and encapsulate the values of its occupants. Embracing the precious commodity of space in the dense urban fabric, the resulting transformer apartments optimised the potential of scarce space to offer creative, modern solutions on par with the luxurious sophistication of the development. By articulating practical storage solutions and adaptive design – such as concealed shelving, pull-out work surfaces, transforming wall beds – in a rigorously detailed presentation, the micro units appeal to urbanites and their desired lifestyle. Guided through deliberate design in altering the interiors to maximise the space of their personal retreats, the occupants are afforded the experience of an urban oasis in a crowded metropolis.

AWARDS

2019 PropertyGuru Vietnam Property Awards
Best Condo Interior Design
(Highly Commended)

SAMSUNG
Premium
UHD TV
55NU8000
HDR ELITE

SAMSUNG
Premium
UHD TV
55NU8000
HDR ELITE
DYNAMIC CRYSTAL COLOR
CLEAN CABLE SOLUTION
ONE REMOTE CONTROL
alpha city

KING PALACE

HANOI, VIETNAM

A modern interpretation of French colonial architecture, the interior design of King Palace in Hanoi blends simplicity with elegance; effectively conveying a sense of timeless sophistication. Within this aesthetic framework, DP Design applied design strategies that reflect on the values and traditions of the local culture and its familial structure, while addressing the question of how the modern development could meet the lifestyle aspirations of homeowners. In creating delightful living spaces that will enliven the spirit, the resultant aesthetic focuses on the facilitation of social connections within community and family through spatial design.

This exploration of design is captured in the show flats, which demonstrate how such a contemporary living experience can be realised in the residential units to potential occupants. The open kitchen concept, for example, has a duplicity of function that goes beyond visual purpose. It ultimately creates an inviting space for communal gathering among family and friends. Through the innovative introduction of a double unit with a communal entrance foyer, the design of King Palace breaks the norms of apartment living to accommodate multi-generational living conventional to Vietnamese culture.

DP Design consistently seeks to address the fundamental questions of how people live, who they are and what they aspire to be. King Palace exemplifies the rigorous process that each project DP Design undertakes, so as to gain critical understanding of its socio-cultural, environmental and economic position. In this manner, DP Design is able to identify issues to be solved by design, taking cues from the users and context to develop cohesive design solutions complemented by clear visual identity.

KING PALACE
NƠI CÁC VỊ VUA SỐNG

FERAZ

MULBERRY LANE & SEASONS AVENUE

HANOI, VIETNAM

Undertaking the show flats for two premier developments in Hanoi, Mulberry Lane and Seasons Avenue respectively, DP Design eschews the archetypal approach of following the latest design trends or exploiting an extreme style to fascinate. Instead the design sought to inspire the question: *Who lives here?*

Briefs were developed for fictional occupants, and each show flat was furnished according to the nominated family's perceived lifestyle and pastimes. The characters of the family are expressed through individualised details and a story unfolds for the prospective buyers as they browse the show flat. Personal items pique interest – a drum set begets the speculation of who the musician in the family is: parent or child? Arresting artwork displays suggest an artistic eye in the family while travel photographs hint at personal memories. In one show flat, the presence of the playful loft bed implies younger children are part of the household; in another, shelves littered with fragile collectibles portray a seemingly itinerant lifestyle. Overlapping the suggested interests with their own, prospective buyers are enthused to see the show flat as their potential home through the intimacy evoked by the personalisation of the living spaces.

Applying such out-of-the-box design strategies, DP Design challenges the perception of how show flats should be conceptualised. It raises the question of whether more can be achieved than focusing on insensible aesthetics centred on prevalent trends. DP Design recognised the key function of a show flat as a life-sized simulation of a future home – regardless of personal tastes and aesthetic preferences, prospective buyers were engaged through a universally appealing showcase of life. The design thought behind the show flats of Mulberry Lane and Seasons Avenue tests time and trend, by speaking to the social aspect of users rather than the physical elements of architecture and interior design.

VISION
MICHAEL JACKSON
London
MONTE CARLO
VISION
VISION
TOO GOOD TO BE TRUE
How Ireland Voted 1989

love

DREAM

OD TO BE TRUE
onal Branding
PHOTO FRAME

RECREATIONAL

CINEMAXX JUNIOR

PALEMBANG, INDONESIA

Cinemaxx Junior encapsulates the ideal cinema-going experience for young families by intuitively integrating the element of play with the movie experience. The novel concept arose from the observation that families with young children often do not fully enjoy their first cinema excursions, where silence is expected and parents spend more time attending to their children. Driven by the objective to accommodate the natural inclinations of children and therefore lessen the stress placed upon parents, an innovative brief was developed for a convergence of physical play and visual entertainment in a functional, cohesively designed setting.

From the commencement of the design, it was sought to holistically implement a truly family-dedicated cinema. The traditional box of the cinema hall was reimagined into a multi-dimensional playground system which permits children to zoom in and out, engaging their innate sense of mobility. Instead of seat assignment in which children are expected to remain immobile for the duration of a show, they are encouraged to explore and socialise in an informal participative space. By so redefining the movie-watching experience, parents and guardians no longer have to worry that their child would be a disturbance to other patrons. This exponentially increases their enjoyment of the space.

The design focus was not confined to the enthrallment of the children; functionality was of utmost importance as a dual strategy for both safety considerations and the ease of parents. The coherently planned layout with generous passageways and zoning for different age groups, enabled easier supervision of mobile children. Other practical applications include sufficient indirect lighting for better visibility, decreased general sound levels in light of the sensitive hearing of young children, a diverse range of age-appropriate play equipment and spacious child-friendly amenities.

The first of its kind in Asia, and breaking new ground in its typology, Cinemaxx Junior is the embodiment of the possibilities in design driven by the desire for a higher quality of social interaction and user experience – a design for humanity.

AWARDS

2016 FX* International Interior Design Awards

IDCS Interior Design Excellence Awards
Public Design
(Gold)

Blueprint Awards
Best Interior Project – Leisure
(Finalist)

WELCOME TO
ULTRA XD
#MAXXperience
Maxximum Movie Experience
www.cinemaxxtheater.com
@cinemaxxtheater
cinemaxx theater

ce
perience
emaxx theater

Comprehensive and in-depth consideration was given to the design in terms of function, aesthetics, ranges of play equipment and lighting with safety at the forefront. Thus, children can enjoy in a fun diverse environment while parents can rest assured.

TUITION
NDP
SUPPORT
PIONEERS

HEARTWARE NETWORK OFFICE

SINGAPORE

Conceptualising the new 350sqm premises, DP's design goal was to create a space of possibilities where youths are able to gather, interact and participate; to be involved. The idea was to break away from the conventional institutional outfit that we see in typical organisations of this nature, and push for a more social response and design, enabling an innovative use of space. The project explored how design can be used as a powerful tool to reach out to the youths of today; to influence the way they reimagine the environment, and identify with place and space while nurturing values within them. These were achieved through the introduction of a distinctive modular and interactive grid furniture system that iterates with various plug-in elements.

A flexible and spontaneous work environment was designed via a customisable canvas with interactive plug-in elements. The distinctive modular and interactive grid furniture system, such as tiered bleachers on wheels, loose seating and individual pedestals, which can be packed away into built-in cabinetry, allows for ideation of spaces, which encourages participation of the youth. Green and smart-control elements incorporated within the space boost youth awareness of the global movement on sustainability and smart technology, therefore also emboldening youths to take ownership of their part for the environment.

While a neutral palette of plywood, white laminate and shades of grey was chosen for the base of the space, accent colours were incorporated, aligning with Heartware Network's corporate colours. An additional overlay of hanging mobiles and signage also add distinctive character to the spaces. Each showcases and advocates the various idealisms that Heartware Network and their youths stand for – doves for authenticity, planes for enterprise, boats for dedication and crane for integrity.

The design of Heartware Network's new office is a reflection of the energy of the youth today; and aims to give the youths who volunteer with the organisation an empowered voice.

AWARDS

2019 IIDA Best of Asia Pacific Design Awards
Corporate Space Small category
(Winner)

Architizer A+ Popular Choice
Concepts – Plus – Architecture + For Good
(Winner)

YOUTHBANK
ekous
THE HALL

ENTERPRISE
IDARE

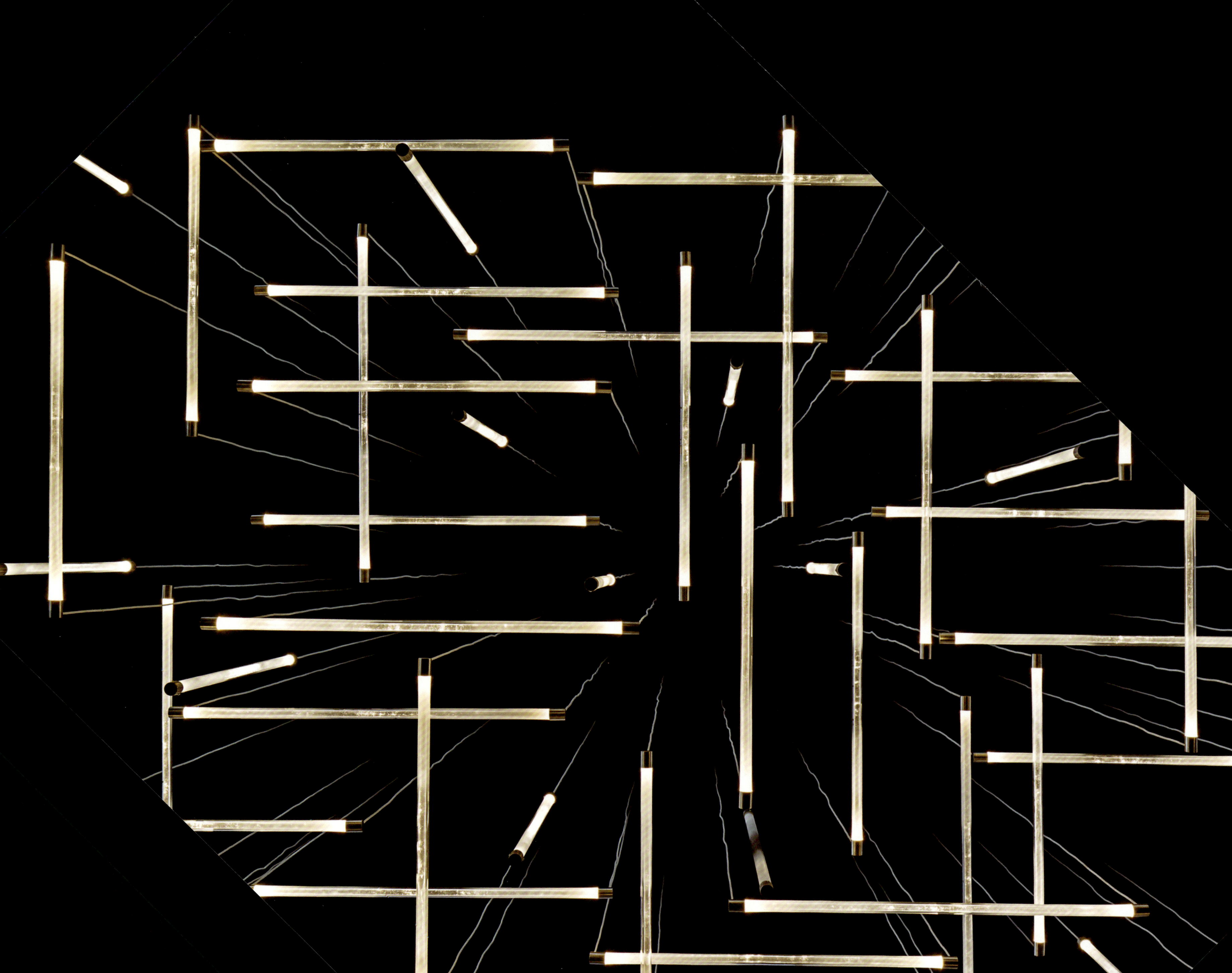

TEMASEK CLUB

SINGAPORE

Nestled among lush foliage at a site adjacent to a nature reserve, Temasek Club was purposed as a sanctuary for Singapore Armed Forces (SAF) Officers to relax within the natural surrounding. Hosting an array of social and recreational facilities, the new clubhouse building spanning 21,000 square metres fulfils the club's vision to be 'The Best Social and Family Club' for the SAF Officers and their families. The design approach holistically addresses the marshal tenets entrenched in the identity of Temasek Club, and the intricacies of elegantly rendering such values in a tranquil and relaxing atmosphere befitting a leisure club.

Sensitive site-planning maximises the potential of the site and prioritises the users' immersive experience in nature. The bulk of the building mass is cleverly concealed in a natural valley in the terrain, allowing for unspoilt views of the nature reserve behind. The architecture and interior design are in perfect harmony through understated yet distinct elements of order, symmetry and hierarchy in rhythmic repetition. These symbolic allusions to the military identity are counterbalanced by the material palette of natural textures and neutral earthy colours.

In alignment with the intent to keep social spaces at the forefront of design consideration, the entrance lobby seamlessly blends into an open-plan F&B establishment showcasing expansive views of the greenery. The main circulation routes are open-to-air in a semi-enclosed naturally ventilated space, anchoring users to the landscape. Similarly, the interior spaces are built to oriente users to the external views, underpinning the strategy to remain intimately connected to the natural backdrop.

Temasek Club exudes a formal and dignified spatial environment while remaining an inviting social and recreational space – an idyllic retreat not overwhelmed by the gravitas of a functional civil service establishment.

TEMASEK GRAND BALLROOM

URBAN ART

CRADLE2CRADLE

SINGAPORE

Inspired by 'Newton's Cradle', our kinetic-light installation blurs the boundaries between science and art.

Through public interaction, the device demonstrates the conservation of momentum and energy using a series of swinging spheres. These same spheres illuminate upon impact and energy transference, resulting in a mesmerising display of light and logic. Through the use of emerging micro-generator technology, kinetic energy produced from the cradles are harnessed to supplement the power required to illuminate the spheres.

Essentially, *Cradle2Cradle* is a power-generating light installation designed to promote public involvement and spread awareness about the global energy problem.

Cradle2Cradle harnesses the rotational and compressive energy generated each time a sphere rolls or collides. Inside each sphere is a custom microgenerator, a pendulum, a Printed Circuit Boards (PCB) that coordinates the process and a rechargeable lithium ion battery. As the sphere moves, the pendulum turns the microgenerator, charging up the battery. Energy stored in the battery is then routed to the Cradle's electrical mainframe, supplying the power required for the lights.

AWARDS

2018 Perspective A&D Trophy Awards
Architecture – Best Pop-up
(Winner)

DRIVEN x DESIGN New York Design Awards
Pop-up Exhibit & Set Design
(Silver)

i light marina bay
Cradle2Cradle
05
05

UBS
OUE

1

2

4

5

7

8

1. Heartware Network Office | Singapore
2. Stephen Riady Centre at NUS UTown | Singapore
3. One Farrer Hotel & Spa | Singapore
4. Ocean Suites at Resort World Sentosa | Singapore
5. The Dubai Mall | Dubai, UAE
6. Esplanade – Theatres on Bay | Singapore
7. Singapore Dance Theatre | Singapore
8. Ngee Ann Polytechnic Block 51 | Singapore
9. Paragon Shopping Centre | Singapore

AWARDS

ALPHA HILL

2019 | PropertyGuru Vietnam Property Awards
Best Condo Interior Design
(Highly Commended)

CINEMAXX JUNIOR

2016 | FX* International Interior Design Awards

2016 | IDCS Interior Design Excellence Awards
Public Design
(Gold)

2016 | Blueprint Awards
Best Interior Project – Leisure
(Finalist)

CRADLE2CRADLE

2018 | Perspective A&D Trophy Awards
Architecture – Best Pop-up
(Winner)

2018 | DRIVEN x DESIGN New York Design Awards
Pop-up Exhibit & Set Design
(Silver)

HEARTWARE NETWORK OFFICE

2019 | IIDA Best of Asia Pacific Design Awards
Corporate Space Small category
(Winner)

2019 | Architizer A+ Popular Choice
Concepts – Plus – Architecture + For Good
(Winner)

LEE KONG CHIAN SCHOOL OF MEDICINE (NOVENA)

2018 | BCI Asia Interior Design Awards
Schools – Singapore
(Winner)

NOVOTEL SINGAPORE ON STEVENS

2019 | IDCS Interior Design Excellence Awards
Best Hospitality Design ≥ 201 Rooms
(Gold)

2018 | BCI Asia Interior Design Award
Hospitality – Singapore
(Winner)

2018 | DRIVEN x DESIGN Melbourne Design Awards
(Gold)

2018 | DRIVEN x DESIGN London Design Awards
Interior Design – International Hospitality
(Silver)

ORCHARD CENTRAL A&A

2015 | Singapore Good Design Mark Awards

OUR TAMPINES HUB

2019 | BCA Universal Design Mark Award
(Platinum)

2018 | DRIVEN x DESIGN London Design Awards
Interior Design – International Public or Institutional
(Silver)

2018 | Global Architecture and Design Awards
(Honourable Mention)

2018 | FX* International Interior Design Awards
(Finalist)

2017 | IDCS Interior Design Excellence Awards
Best Public Design – Asia Pacific
(Silver)

2017 | BCA Universal Design Mark Award
(GoldPLUS)

PERENNIAL INTERNATIONAL MEDICAL CENTRE

2018 | IIDA Best of Asia Pacific Design Awards
Healthcare
(Winner)

REDPAN

2017 | Prix Versailles
Asie du Sud et Pacifique Restaurants

2016 | IDCS Interior Design Excellence Awards
– F&B Design
(Bronze)

YOTEL SINGAPORE

2019 | IDCS Interior Design Excellence Awards
Best Hospitality Design ≥ 201 Rooms
(Silver)

2018 | BCI Asia Interior Design Awards
Hospitality
(Merit)

DP DESIGN PTE LTD

2019 | Singapore Design Awards
Corporate Place-making
(Finalist)

2019 | IDCS Interior Design Excellence Awards
– Top 3 ID Firm of the Year
(Silver)

FUTURE PROJECTS

Designing for future needs and tastes is a challenge that all designers undertake. With the digital age in full flux, it is fast changing the way we interact; thus, affecting the manner in which we perceive and utilise space as individuals and as a community. At the core, however, a well-designed interior continues to be defined by its ability to delight users, to facilitate fellowship, to influence behaviour and to adapt to change. From the client's perspective, a well-designed interior continues to be characterised by how it adds value and gives a unique identity to the property.

In light of this, it is no longer enough to simply distinguish a project from its contemporaries. Designers must understand the macro socio-economic perspective and all its accompanying nuances. Thus, in aspiring to break through the boundaries of today, our designs of tomorrow will incorporate new materials and technologies so as to better shape public spaces and enrich user experience.

COURTYARD MARRIOTT
HOSPITALITY | DANANG, VIETNAM

FRASER RESIDENCES
HOSPITALITY | HANOI, VIETNAM

FRASER SUITES HANOI
HOSPITALITY | HANOI, VIETNAM

HI LAI HOTEL
HOSPITALITY | TAIPEI, TAIWAN

MARRIOTT HOTEL AT GOLDEN SQUARE
HOSPITALITY | DANANG, VIETNAM

MILLENNIUM HOTEL LONDON KNIGHTSBRIDGE
HOSPITALITY | LONDON, UNITED KINGDOM

OAKWOOD HOTEL AND APARTMENTS
HOSPITALITY | YANGON, MYANMAR

SIX STAR LUXURY HOTEL
HOSPITALITY | LUSAIL, QATAR

TRANS HOTEL MERCURE
HOSPITALITY | JAKARTA, INDONESIA

TRAVELODGE HARBOURFRONT
HOSPITALITY | SINGAPORE

FICO TOWER
RESIDENTIAL | HO CHI MINH CITY, VIETNAM

5ONE CENTRAL
RETAIL | SINGAPORE

ASSIMA PROJECT
RETAIL | KUWAIT CITY, KUWAIT

CLEOPATRA MALL
RETAIL | CAIRO, EGYPT

HEARTLAND 66
RETAIL | WUHAN, CHINA

JEM A&A
RETAIL | SINGAPORE

KLCC MALL
RETAIL | KUALA LUMPUR, MALAYSIA

MALL OF RABAT
RETAIL | RABAT, MOROCCO

MANDALAY HUB RETAIL MALL
RETAIL | MANDALAY, MYANMAR

MARRAKECH MALL
RETAIL | MARRAKECH, MOROCCO

THE EXCHANGE TRX
RETAIL | KUALA LUMPUR, MALAYSIA

THE LIGHT CITY
RETAIL | PENANG, MALAYSIA

THOMSON PLAZA A&A
RETAIL | SINGAPORE

WESTSIDE CITY RESORTS WORLD
RETAIL | MANILA, PHILIPPINES

DP50 X SUPERMAMA

A LIMITED EDITION FOR OUR GOLDEN JUBILEE

In 2017, DP commemorated five decades of design excellence; and as part of its golden jubilee, the firm released a set of limited edition plates featuring iconic architecture from its portfolio of works. They are, namely, Esplanade – Theatres on the Bay, Singapore Sports Hub, The Dubai Mall and The Orchard Road Experience.

The collection, designed by DP Design, was both an ode to the meaningful public spaces DP has conceptualised as well as a celebration of its design milestones over the years. Produced in collaboration with Supermama, the collection was crafted on classic white porcelain and in signature blue prints – symbolic of DP's home-grown roots and growing international purview; and an expression of DP's continued dedication towards design of uncompromising quality.

The Dubai Mall

Esplanade - Theatres on the Bay

Esplanade - Theatres on the Bay

Orchard Road Experience

Singapore Sports Hub

Singapore Sports Hub

BEHIND THE SCENES

DP Design is made up of a group of dedicated designers from diverse backgrounds, trained in both architecture and interior design, locally and internationally. Our people are our greatest asset – they define our ability to serve our clients. For this reason, we are committed to developing the talent, creativity and competency of our people.

The firm operates on a studio-team basis, covering a full range of typologies such as hospitality, retail and institutional. There is an open and collaborative culture within the firm, which encourages everyone from a junior designer to a senior associate to be a hands-on contributor and confidently share ideas and opinions. Interaction with our leaders and design-sharing sessions help to cultivate teamwork and trust, as well as a sense of ownership and pride in our work.

Within the office, a carefully curated library of design periodicals and publications, including a wide range of material samples, has been set up to facilitate the sharing of knowledge within the team. There is a constant effort to keep up with new materials and applications in the market so as to produce a diverse portfolio of work that meets the unique needs of our global client base.

DPA

DELL
MARCUS

ABOUT DP ARCHITECTS

& ITS GROUP OF COMPANIES

Founded in 1967, DP Architects is a leading architecture practice in Asia with 1,100 staff in 16 global offices. The firm has been involved with urban projects of immense scale and increasing diversity of function for over five decades, and approaches each project as the continuation of an ongoing exploration in shaping the public domain.

During five decades of continuous growth, DP Architects has evolved into an industry-leading, multidisciplinary design practice that operates as the DPA group of companies. DP Consultants, DP Design, DP Engineers, DP Facade, DP Green, DP Lighting, DP Sustainable Design and DP Urban complement DP Architects to deliver fully coordinated, innovative design solutions at all scales.

The firm's recent architectural works are some of the largest of their type in the world: Singapore Sports Hub, the world's largest hub ecosystem of its kind that bridges sports and community, with venues that cater to world-class sporting events and everyday participation; The Dubai Mall, a 'city within a city' measuring 550,000 square metres hosting programmes of shopping, entertainment and leisure, and was in 2015 one of the world's most visited leisure destination with 92 million visitors; Resorts World Sentosa, a $6.5 billion mixed-use complex in Singapore, comprising a Universal Studios theme park, a marine life park, a maritime museum, a casino and six hotels; Esplanade – Theatres on the Bay, a national icon and the civic heart of Singapore that was designed and constructed over a decade, and named as one of the world's 15 most beautiful concert halls; and a series of some 30 retail mall projects along Singapore's Orchard Road that redeveloped an entire shopping corridor.

While many of the firm's works have their roots in Singapore, the ideas and techniques of the firm have expanded to projects overseas. As a practice ingrained with a special understanding of regional progress and needs, DPA applies this regional knowledge – from aspects of climate to social and economic factors that contribute to a city's long-term health – to its projects throughout Asia, the Middle East and beyond.

1

OUR TAMPINES HUB

2

EMAAR

5

NOVOTEL
N
Mercure

6

Sengkang
Community
Hospital

10

THEADDRESS

3

4

7

8

9

11

1. Our Tampines Hub | Singapore

2. Emaar Square Mall | Istanbul, Turkey

3. SingPost Centre | Singapore

4. 8 Saint Thomas | Singapore

5. Novotel Singapore on Stevens | Singapore

6. Sengkang Hospital Campus | Singapore

7. Frasers Tower | Singapore

8. Yotel Singapore | Singapore

9. Lee Kong Chian School of Medicine | Singapore

10. The Dubai Mall | Dubai, UAE

11. Temasek Club | Singapore

CREDITS

ACKNOWLEGDEMENTS

This book would not be complete without the contributions of colleagues in DP Design. We are always grateful for the early lessons imparted and the firm foundations that our preceding directors have set us on.

To each and every DPian, current and former, thank you for your dedication of time, ideas, effort and knowledge in our collective pursuit of design excellence and commitment to the people we design for.

We would also like to express our gratitude to DP Architects, its board of directors and the DPA group of companies. This book is in part a product of the unique and dynamic design partnership we share; and would not have been possible without your support.

CLIENTS

Al Futtaim Investment Management Limited
Alpha King Real Estate Development Joint Stock Company
Chengdu Ruifeng Commercial Real Estate Co., Ltd
DP Life Pte Ltd
Emaar Properties PJSC
Frasers Hospitality Group Pte Ltd
Gelso Vietnam Joint Stock Company
Heartware Network
Kienta Engineering Construction Pte Ltd
Lendlease Singapore Pte Ltd
Ministry of Health
Nanyang Technological University
Orchard Central Pte Ltd
Orchard Turn Retail Investment Pte Ltd
Oxley Gem Pte Ltd
Pico Pro Pte Ltd
PT Cinemaxx
Sakura Real Estate Joint Stock Company
Shaw House Pte Ltd
Singapore Airlines Limited
Singapore Post Ltd
Sunray Vietnam Company Limited
Trans Property
Yat Yuen Hong Co Ltd

EDITOR-IN-CHIEF

Angelene Chan
Mike Lim

EDITORIAL TEAM

Belle Chung
Win Le Htun
Josy Koh
Christopher Chia

GRAPHICS EDITOR

Rebecca Jin

LAYOUT & COVER DESIGN

Rebecca Jin

IMAGE CREDITS - PHOTOGRAPHERS

Marc Tey

Bahr Karim - Page 246, The Dubai Mall

Christopher O'Grady - Page 108-109, 115, Yotel Singapore

Dominique Savio - Page 100, 102-105, Singapore Airlines SilverKris Lounge

Juliana Tan - Page 6, Foreword; Page 240-243, Behind the Scenes

Pocholo Mauricio - Page 68, 70-71, SingPost Centre

Studio Periphery - Page 122-125, 127-129, Lee Kong Chian School of Medicine; Page 132-135, 138, 140-141, Tampines Regional Library at OTH

CONTACT DETAILS

DP DESIGN PTE LTD
6 Raffles Boulevard
#02-249 Marina Square
Singapore 039594
T +65 6338 3988 F +65 6337 9989
dpdesign@dpdesign.com.sg

DP ARCHITECTS PTE LTD
dparchitects@dpa.com.sg

DP CONSULTANTS
dpconsultants@dpc.com.sg

DP ENGINEERS
dpengineers@dpe.com.sg

DP FAÇADE
dpf@dpfacade.com.sg

DP GREEN
dpgreen@dpg.com.sg

DP LIGHTING
dplighting@dplighting.com.sg

DP SUSTAINABLE DESIGN
dpsd@dpsd.com.sg

DP URBAN
dpurban@dpurban.com.sg

CHINA
DP ARCHITECTS PTE LTD
(SHANGHAI)
Unit 601, Block 11, Mengzhi Park
207 Mengzi Road
Huangpu District
Shanghai 200023
shanghai@dpa.com.sg

DP ARCHITECTS PTE LTD
(Shenzhen Branch)
R016, 41/F, Block A
KK100 Building, No 5016
Shennan East Road, Luohu District
Shenzhen 518001
shenzhen@dpa.com.sg

DP ARCHITECTS PTE LTD
(Guangzhou Branch)
Unit 1002 Tower A
No 157 Linhe Road West
Tian'he District
Guangzhou 510610
guangzhou@dpa.com.sg

INDIA
DPA CONSULTANTS PVT LTD
(Mumbai Branch)
76, 7th Floor Free Press House 215
Nariman Point
Mumbai 400 021
mumbai@dpaconsultants.in

DPA CONSULTANTS PVT LTD
(Bengaluru Branch)
27/1, 4th Cross
5th Main Jayamahal Extension
Bengaluru 560 046
bengaluru@dpaconsultants.in

INDONESIA
PT DP ARCHITECTS INDONESIA
One Pacific Place, Level 11
Sudriman Central Business District,
Jalan Jenderal Sudirman Kav. 52-53
Jakarta 12190
jakarta@dpa.com.sg

MALAYSIA
DP ARCHITECTS SDN BHD
(Kuala Lumpur Branch)
Level 20 AMODA, 22 Jalan Imbi
55100 Kuala Lumpur
kualalumpur@dpa.com.sg

DP ARCHITECTS SDN BHD
(Johor Bahru Branch)
Suite 22.06, Level 22
Johor Bahru City Square
Jalan Wong Ah Fook
80000 Johor Bahru
johorbahru@dpa.com.sg

DPE CONSULTANTS SDN BHD
Level 20 AMODA, 22 Jalan Imbi
55100 Kuala Lumpur
dpe@dpengineers.com.my

MYANMAR
DP ARCHITECTS PTE LTD
(Myanmar Branch)
No. 3/A Bogyoke Aung San Road
Suite 33, #14-00
Junction City Office Tower
Pabedan Township
Yangon 11143
yangon@dpa.com.sg

THAILAND
DP ARCHITECTS (THAILAND) LTD
(Thailand Branch)
No. 44 Smooth Life Tower
Unit No. 1502, 15th Floor
North Sathorn Road, Bang Rak,
Bangkok 10500
bangkok@dpa.com.sg

TURKEY
DP ARCHITECTS PTE LTD
(Turkey Branch)
Buyukdere Caddesi
No:201 K:6 D:101, Levent 34394
Besiktas, Istanbul
istanbul@dpa.com.sg

UNITED ARAB EMIRATES
DP ARCHITECTS PTE LTD
(Dubai Branch)
Nassima Tower Office 1103
Trade Centre 1 Sheikh Zayed Road
PO Box 211711, Dubai
dubai@dpa.com.sg

UNITED KINGDOM
DP INTERNATIONAL (UK) LTD
38-39 St John's Lane
Farringdon, London
EC1M 4BJ
london@dpa.com.sg

VIETNAM
DP ARCHITECTS VIETNAM CO., LTD
(Hanoi Branch)
Cogo CoWorking
TNR Tower (Vincom), Level 16
No. 54A Nguyen Chi Thanh Street
Dong Da District, Hanoi
hanoi@dpa.com.sg

DP ARCHITECTS VIETNAM CO., LTD
(Ho Chi Minh City Branch)
Unit 22-120, Level 22
WeWork E Town Central
11 Doan Van Bo, Ward 12, District 4
Ho Chi Minh City
hochiminhcity@dpa.com.sg